The Hidden Mysteries of Christianity

By Annie Besant

Copyright © 2021 Lamp of Trismegistus. All rights reserved. No part of this publication may be reproduced or transmitted in any form or by any means, electronic or mechanical, including photocopying, recording, or by any information storage and retrieval system, without permission in writing from Lamp of Trismegistus. Reviewers may quote brief passages.

ISBN: 978-1-63118-534-2

Esoteric Classics

Other Books in this Series and Related Titles

The Use of Evil by Annie Besant (978-1-63118-532-8)

Aurora of the Philosophers by Paracelsus (978-1-63118-507-6)

The Historic, Mythic and Mystic Christ by Annie Besant (978–1–63118–533–5)

Clairvoyance and Psychic Abilities by A Besant &c (978-1-63118-403-1)

The Feminine Occult by various authors (978-1-63118-711-7)

Rosicrucian Rules, Secret Signs, Codes and Symbols by various (978-1-63118-488-8)

An Outline of Theosophy by C W Leadbeater (978-1-63118-452-9)

Paracelsus, the Four Elements and Their Spirits by M P Hall (978-1-63118-400-0)

The Stone of the Philosophers by A E Waite (978-1-63118-509-0)

Essays on the Esoteric Tradition of Karma by A Besant &c (978-1-63118-426-0)

The Rosicrucian Chemical Marriage by Christian Rosenkreuz (978-1-63118-458-1)

The Alchemical Catechism of Paracelsus by Paracelsus (978-1-63118-513-7)

Alchemy in the Nineteenth Century by Helena P Blavatsky (978-1-63118-446-8)

Qabbalistic Teachings and the Tree of Life by M P Hall (978-1-63118-482-6)

History, Analysis and Secret Tradition of the Tarot by Hall &c (978-1-63118-445-1)

Crystal Vision Through Crystal Gazing by Frater Achad (978-1-63118-455-0)

The Golden Verses of Pythagoras: Five Translations (978-1-63118-479-6)

Arcane Formulas or Mental Alchemy by W W Atkinson (978-1-63118-459-8)

The Machinery of the Mind by Dion Fortune (978-1-63118-451-2)

The A E Waite Reader: A Selection of Occult Essays (978-1-63118-515-1)

The Leadbeater Reader: A Selection of Occult Essays (978-1-63118-483-3)

Audio versions are also available on Audible, Amazon and Apple

Other Books in this Series and Related Titles

On the Cave of the Nymphs in the Odyssey by Thomas Taylor (978-1-63118-505-2)

Occult Symbolism of Animals, Insects, Reptiles, Fish & Birds (978-1-63118-420-8)

The Poem of Hashish by A Crowley & C Baudelaire (978-1-63118-484-0)

Brothers & Builders by Joseph Fort Newton (978-1-63118-506-9)

The Kabbalah of Masonry & Related Writings by E Levi &c (978-1-63118-453-6)

A Collection of Fiction and Essays by Occult Writers on Supernatural and Metaphysical Subjects by various (978–1–63118–510–6)

The Sepher Yetzirah and the Qabalah by M P Hall (978-1-63118-481-9)

Cloud Upon the Sanctuary by Waite & K Eckartshausen (978-1-63118-438-3)

The Hymns of Hermes by G R S Mead (978-1-63118-405-5)

The Secrets of Enoch by Enoch (978-1-63118-449-9)

Masonic and Rosicrucian History by M P Hall & H Voorhis (978-1-63118-486-4)

The Devil in Love by Jacques Cazotte (978–1–63118–499–4)

The Eleusinian Mysteries and Rites by Dudley Wright (978–1–63118–530–4)

Gnosis of the Mind by G. R. S. Mead (978-1-63118-408-6)

The First and Second Gospels of the Infancy of Jesus Christ (978-1-63118-415-4)

The Life of Pythagoras by Porphyry (978-1-63118-512-0)

Freemasonry & Catholicism by Max Heindel (978-1-63118-508-3)

Rosicrucians and Speculative Masonry in the Seventeenth Century (978-1-63118-489-5)

The Influence of Pythagoras on Freemasonry and Other Essays (978-1-63118-404-8)

The Path of Light: A Manual of Maha-Yana Buddhism (978-1-63118-471-0)

Tao Te Ching & Commentary by Lao Tzu & C Johnston (978-1-63118-495-6)

Audio versions are also available on Audible, Amazon and Apple

Table of Contents

Introduction…7

The Hidden Mysteries of Christianity

Part I: Testimony of the Scriptures…9

Part II: Testimony of the Church…27

INTRODUCTION

The word "esoteric" can be difficult to define. Esotericism in general can be seen less as a system of beliefs and more as a category, which encompasses numerous, different systems of beliefs. It's a bit of juxtaposition, since the word "esoteric" indicates something that few people know about, while the term itself broadly covers numerous philosophies, practices, areas of study and belief systems.

In a greater sense, Esotericism acts as a storehouse for secret knowledge, which is often considered ancient (by *tradition, if not by fact),* passed down from generation to generation, in private. At various times in history, simply possessing the knowledge of some of these subjects, was considered illegal and a jailable offence, if discovered. This usually included such general topics as Alchemy, Pharmacology, Qabalah, Hermeticism, Occultism, Ceremonial Magic, Astrology, Divination, Rosicrucianism and so on. Collectively, these areas of study were often referred to as the esoteric sciences.

Sometimes, the outer garment of a subject isn't esoteric, while what is hidden beneath it, is. As an example, Freemasonry isn't necessarily esoteric by nature (at *least not anymore),* but certain signs, passwords and handshakes given to the candidate during their initiation, are in fact, esoteric, in the sense that they are hidden from the general public.

Today, in the twenty-first century, such topics are readily available at bookstores across the country, and numerous mainsteam publishers offer beginners guides and coffee-table volumes on many of these subjects, intended for mass appeal. Books like *"The Secret"* have turned previously arcane topics into household knowledge. All that being the case, however, it isn't to say that there still aren't buried secrets to uncover, ancient wisdom being ignored and forgotten mysteries to be explored. In fact, it is often that we are only able to further our own studies by standing on the shoulders of these disappearing giants.

Lamp of Trismegistus is doing its part to help preserve humanity's esoteric history by making some of these classics available to those students who are seeking to unearth the knowledge of these ancient colossi.

So, be sure to check other titles from our *Esoteric Classics* series, as well as our *Occult Fiction, Theosophical Classics, Foundations of Freemasonry Series, Supernatural Fiction, Paranormal Research Series, Studies in Buddhism* and our *Christian Apocrypha Series.* You can also download the audio versions of most of these titles from Amazon, Apple or Audible, for learning on the go.

THE HIDDEN MYSTERIES OF CHRISTIANITY

PART I

THE TESTIMONY OF THE SCRIPTURES

Having seen that the religions of the past claimed with one voice to have a hidden side, to be custodians of "Mysteries", and that this claim was endorsed by the seeking of initiation by the greatest men, we must now ascertain whether Christianity stands outside this circle of religions, and alone is without a Gnosis, offering to the world only a simple faith and not a profound knowledge. Were it so, it would indeed be a sad and lamentable fact, proving Christianity to be intended for a class only, and not for all types of human beings. But that it is not so, we shall be able to prove beyond the possibility of rational doubt.

And that proof is the thing which Christendom at this time most sorely needs, for the very flower of Christendom is perishing for lack of knowledge. If the esoteric teaching can be re-established and win patient and earnest students, it will not be long before the occult is also restored. Disciples of the Lesser Mysteries will become candidates for the Greater, and with the regaining of knowledge will come again the authority of teaching. And truly the need is great. For, looking at the world around us, we find that religion in the West is suffering from the very difficulty that theoretically we should expect to find. Christianity, having lost its mystic and esoteric teaching, is losing its hold on a large number of the more highly educated, and the partial revival during the past few years is coincident with the re-introduction of some mystic teaching. It is patent to every student of the closing forty years of the last century, that crowds of thoughtful and moral people have slipped away from the churches, because the teachings they received there outraged their intelligence and shocked their moral sense. It is idle to pretend that the widespread agnosticism of this period had its root either in lack of morality or in deliberate crookedness of mind. Everyone who carefully studies the phenomena presented will admit that men of strong intellect have been driven out of Christianity by the crudity of the religious ideas set before them, the contradictions in the authoritative teachings, the views as to God, man, and the universe that no trained intelligence could possibly admit. Nor can it be said that any kind of moral degradation lay at the root of the revolt against the dogmas of the Church. The rebels were not too bad for their religion; on the contrary, it was the religion that was too bad for them. The rebellion against popular Christianity was due to the awakening and the growth of conscience; it was the conscience that revolted, as well as the intelligence, against teachings dishonouring to God and man alike, that represented God as a tyrant, and man as essentially evil, gaining salvation by slavish submission.

The reason for this revolt lay in the gradual descent of Christian teaching into so-called simplicity, so that the most ignorant might be able to grasp it. Protestant religionists asserted loudly that nothing ought to be preached save that which every one could grasp, that the glory of the Gospel lay in its simplicity, and that the child and the unlearned ought to be able to understand and apply it to life. True enough, if by this it were meant that there are some religious truths that all can grasp, and that a religion fails if it leaves the lowest, the most ignorant, the most dull, outside the pale of its elevating influence. But false, utterly false, if by this it be meant that religion has no truths that the ignorant cannot understand, that it is so poor and limited a thing that it has nothing to teach which is above the thought of the unintelligent or above the moral purview of the degraded. False, fatally false, if such be the meaning; for as that view spreads, occupying the pulpits and being sounded in the churches, many noble men and women, whose hearts are half-broken as they sever the links that bind them to their early faith, withdraw from the churches, and leave their places to be filled by the hypocritical and the ignorant. They pass either into a state of passive agnosticism, or — if they be young and enthusiastic — into a condition of active aggression, not believing that that can be the highest which outrages alike intellect and conscience, and preferring the honesty of open unbelief to the drugging of the intellect and the conscience at the bidding of an authority in which they recognise nothing that is divine.

In thus studying the thought of our time we see that the question of a hidden teaching in connection with Christianity becomes of vital importance. Is Christianity to survive as the religion of the West ? Is it to live through the centuries of the future, and to continue to play a part in moulding the thought of the evolving western races ? If it is to live, it must regain the knowledge it has lost, and again have its mystic and its occult teachings; it must again stand forth as an authoritative teacher of spiritual verities, clothed with the only authority worth anything, the authority of knowledge. If these teachings be regained, their influence will soon be seen in wider and deeper views of truth; dogmas, which now seem like mere shells and fetters, shall again be seen to be partial presentments of fundamental realities. First, Esoteric Christianity will reappear in the " Holy Place", in the Temple, so that all who are capable of receiving it may follow its lines of published thought; and secondly, Occult Christianity will again descend into the Adytum, dwelling behind the Veil which guards the "Holy of Holies", into which only the Initiate may enter. Then again will occult teaching be within the reach of those who qualify themselves to receive it, according to the ancient rules, those who are willing in modern days to meet the ancient demands, made on all those who would fain know the reality and truth of spiritual things.

Once again we turn our eyes to history, to see whether Christianity was unique among religions in having no inner teaching, or whether it resembled all others in possessing this hidden treasure. Such a question is a matter of evidence, not of theory, and must be decided by the authority of the existing documents and not by the mere ipse dixit of modern Christians.

As a matter of fact both the "New Testament" and the writings of the early Church make the same declarations as to the possession by the Church of such teachings, and we learn from these the fact of the existence of Mysteries — called the Mysteries of Jesus, or the Mystery of the Kingdom — the conditions imposed on candidates, something of the general nature of the teachings given, and other details. Certain passages in the "New Testament" would remain entirely obscure, if it were not for the light thrown on them by the definite statements of the Fathers and Bishops of the Church, but in that light they became clear and intelligible.

It would indeed have been strange had it been otherwise when we consider the lines of religious thought which influenced primitive Christianity. Allied to the Hebrews, the Persians, and the Greeks, tinged by the older faiths of India, deeply coloured by Syrian and Egyptian thought, this later branch of the great religious stem could not do other than again re-affirm the ancient traditions, and place in the grasp of western races the full treasure of the ancient teaching. "The faith once delivered to the saints" would indeed have been shorn of its chief value if, when delivered to the West, the pearl of esoteric teaching had been withheld.

The first evidence to be examined is that of the "New Testament". For our purpose we may put aside all the vexed questions of different readings and different authors, that can only be decided by scholars. Critical scholarship has much to say on the age of MSS., on the authenticity of documents, and so on. But we need not concern ourselves with these. We may accept the canonical Scriptures, as showing what was believed in the early Church as to the teaching of the Christ and of His immediate followers, and see what they say as to the existence of a secret teaching given only to the few. Having seen the words put into the mouth of Jesus Himself, and regarded by the Church as of supreme authority, we will look at the writings of the great apostle S. Paul; then we will consider the statements made by those who inherited the apostolic tradition and guided the Church during the first centuries A.D. Along this unbroken line of tradition and written testimony the proposition that Christianity had a hidden side can be established. We shall further find that the Lesser Mysteries of mystic interpretation can be traced through the centuries to the beginning of the 19th century, and that though there were no Schools of Mysticism recognised as preparatory to Initiation, after the disappearance of the Mysteries, yet great Mystics, from time to time, reached the lower stages of ecstasy, by their own sustained efforts, aided doubtless by invisible Teachers.

The words of the Master Himself are clear and definite, and were, as we shall see, quoted by Origen as referring to the secret teaching preserved in the Church. "And when he was alone, they that were about Him with the twelve asked of Him the parable. And He said unto them, 'Unto you it is given to know the mystery of the kingdom of God, but unto them that are without, all these things are done in parables'. And later: "With many such parables spake He the word unto them, as they were able to hear it. But without a parable spake He not unto them; and when they were alone He expounded all things to His disciples". Mark the significant words, "when they were alone", and the phrase, "them that are without". So also in the version of S. Matthew: "Jesus sent the multitude away, and went into the house; and His disciples came unto Him". These teachings given "in the house", the innermost meanings of His instructions, were alleged to be handed on from teacher to teacher. The Gospel gives, it will be noted, the allegorical mystic explanation, that which we have called The Lesser Mysteries, but the deeper meaning was said to be given only to the Initiates.

Again, Jesus tells even His apostles: "I have yet many things to say to you, but ye cannot bear them now". Some of them were probably said after His death, when He was seen of His disciples, "speaking of the things pertaining to the kingdom of God". None of these have been publicly recorded, but who can believe that they were neglected or forgotten, and were not handed down as a priceless possession ? There was a tradition in the Church that He visited His apostles for a considerable period after His death, for the sake of giving them instruction — a fact that will be referred to later — and in the famous Gnostic treatise, the Pistis Sophia, we read: "It came to pass, when Jesus had risen from the dead, that He passed eleven years speaking with His disciples and instructing them". Then there is the phrase, which many would fain soften and explain away: "Give not that which is holy to the dogs, neither cast ye your pearls before swine" — a precept which is of general application indeed, but was considered by the early Church to refer to the secret teachings. It should be remembered that the words had not the same harshness of sound in the ancient days as they have now; for the word "dogs" — like "the vulgar", "the profane" — was applied by those within a certain circle to all who were outside its pale, whether by a society or association, or by a nation —as by the Jews to all Gentiles. It was sometimes used to designate those who were outside the circle of Initiates, and we find it employed in that sense in the early Church; those who, not having been initiated into the Mysteries, were regarded as being outside "the kingdom of God", or " the spiritual Israel", had this name applied to them.

There were several names, exclusive of the term "The Mystery", or "The Mysteries", used to designate the sacred circle of the Initiates or connected with Initiation: "The Kingdom", "The Kingdom of God", "The Kingdom of Heaven", "The Narrow Path", "The Strait Gate", "The Perfect", "The Saved", "Life Eternal", "Life", "The Second Birth", "A Little One", "A Little Child". The meaning is made plain by the use of these words in early Christian writings, and in some cases even outside the Christian pale. Thus the term, "The Perfect", was used by the Essenes, who had three orders in their communities: the Neophytes, the Brethren, and the Perfect — the latter being Initiates; and it is employed generally in that sense in old writings. "The Little Child" was the ordinary name for a candidate just initiated, i.e., who had just taken his "second birth".

When we know this use, many obscure and otherwise harsh passages become intelligible "Then said one unto Him: Lord, are there few that be saved ? And He said unto them: Strive to enter in at the strait gate; for many, I say unto you, will seek to enter in and shall not be able". If this be applied in the ordinary Protestant way to salvation from everlasting hell-fire, the statement becomes incredible, shocking. No Saviour of the world can be supposed to assert that many will seek to avoid hell and enter heaven, but will not be able to do so. But as applied to the narrow gateway of Initiation and to salvation from rebirth, it is perfectly true and natural. So again: "Enter ye in at the strait gate; for wide is the gate and broad is the way that leadeth to destruction, and many there be which go in thereat; because strait is the gate and narrow is the way which leadeth unto life; and few there be that find it". The warning which immediately follows against the false prophets, the teachers of the dark Mysteries, is most apposite in this connection. No student can miss the familiar ring of these words used in this same sense in other writings. The "ancient narrow way" is familiar to all; the path "difficult to tread as the sharp edge of a razor", already mentioned; the going "from death to death" of those who follow the flower-strewn path of desires, who do not know God; for those men only become immortal and escape from the wide mouth of death, from ever repeated destruction, who have quitted all desires. The allusion to death is, of course, to the repeated births of the soul into gross material existence, regarded always as "death" compared to the "life" of the higher and subtler worlds.

This "Strait Gate" was the gateway of Initiation, and through it a candidate entered "The Kingdom". And it ever has been, and must be, true that only a few can enter that gateway, though myriads — an exceedingly "great multitude, which no man could number", not a few — enter into the happiness of the heaven-world. So also spoke another great Teacher, nearly three thousand years earlier: "Among thousands of men scarce one striveth for perfection; of the successful strivers scarce one knoweth me in essence". For the Initiates are few in each generation, the flower of humanity; but no gloomy sentence of everlasting woe is pronounced in this statement on the vast majority of the human race. The saved are, as Proclus taught, hose who escape from the circle of generation, within which humanity is bound.

In this connection we may recall the story of the young man who came to Jesus, and, addressing Him as "Good Master", asked how he might win eternal life — the well-recognised liberation from rebirth by knowledge of God. His first answer was the regular exoteric precept: "Keep the commandments". But when the young man answered: "All these things have I kept from my youth up"; then, to that conscience free from all knowledge of transgression, came the answer of the true Teacher: "If thou wilt be perfect, go and sell that thou hast, and give to the poor, and thou shalt have treasure in heaven; and come and follow me". "If thou wilt be perfect", be a member of the Kingdom, poverty and obedience must be embraced. And then to His own disciples Jesus explains that a rich man can hardly enter the Kingdom of Heaven, such entrance being more difficult than for a camel to pass through the eye of a needle; with men such entrance could not be, with God all things were possible. Only God in man can pass that barrier.

This text has been variously explained away, it being obviously impossible to take it in its surface meaning, that a rich man cannot enter a post-mortem state of happiness. Into that state the rich man may enter as well as the poor, and the universal practice of Christians shows that they do not for one moment believe that riches imperil their happiness after death. But if the real meaning of the Kingdom of Heaven be taken, we have the expression of a simple and direct fact. For that knowledge of God which is Eternal Life cannot be gained till everything earthly is surrendered, cannot be learned until everything has been sacrificed. The man must give up not only earthly wealth, which henceforth may only pass through his hands as steward, but he must give up his inner wealth as well, so far as he holds it as his own against the world; until he is stripped naked he cannot pass the narrow gateway. Such has ever been a condition of Initiation, and "poverty, obedience, chastity", has been the vow of the candidate.

The "second birth" is another well-recognised term for Initiation; even now in India the higher castes are called "twice-born", and the ceremony that makes them twice-born is a ceremony of Initiation — mere husk truly, in these modern days, but the "pattern of things in the heavens". When Jesus is speaking to Nicodemus, He states that "Except a man be born again, he cannot see the kingdom of God", and this birth is spoken of as that "of water and the Spirit", this is the first Initiation; a later one is that of "the Holy Ghost and fire", the baptism of the Initiate in his manhood, as the first is that of birth, which welcomes him as "the Little Child" entering the Kingdom. How thoroughly this imagery was familiar among the mystics of the Jews is shown by the surprise evinced by Jesus when Nicodemus stumbled over His mystic phraseology: "Art thou a master of Israel, and knowest not these things?"

Another precept of Jesus which remains as "a hard saying" to his followers is: "Be ye therefore perfect, even as your Father which is in heaven is perfect". The ordinary Christian knows that he cannot possibly obey this command; full of ordinary human frailties and weaknesses, how can he become perfect as God is perfect? Seeing the impossibility of the achievement set before him, he quietly puts it aside, and thinks no more about it. But seen as the crowning effort of many lives of steady improvement, as the triumph of the God within us over the lower nature, it comes within calculable distance, and we recall the words of Porphyry, how the man who achieves " the paradigmatic virtues is the Father of the Gods", and that in the Mysteries these virtues were acquired.

S. Paul follows in the footsteps of his Master, and speaks in exactly the same sense, but, as might be expected from his organising work in the Church, with greater explicitness and clearness. The student should read with attention chapters ii. and iii. and verse 1 of chapter iv. of the First Epistle to the Corinthians, remembering, as he reads, that the words are addressed to baptised and communicant members of the Church, full members from the modern standpoint, although described as babes and carnal by the Apostle. They were not catechumens or neophytes, but men and women who were in complete possession of all the privileges and responsibilities of Church membership, recognised by the Apostle as being separate from the world, and expected not to behave as men of the world. They were, in fact, in possession of all that the modern Church gives to its members. Let us summarise the Apostle's words:

"I came to you bearing the divine testimony, not alluring you with human wisdom but with the power of the Spirit. Truly ' we speak wisdom among them that are perfect but it is no human wisdom. ' We speak the wisdom of God in a mystery, even the hidden wisdom, which God ordained before the world' began, and which none even of the princes of this world know. The things of that wisdom are beyond men's thinking, 'but God hath revealed them unto us by his Spirit . . the deep things of God'. 'which the Holy Ghost teacheth'. These are spiritual things, to be discerned only by the spiritual man, in whom is the mind of Christ. ' And I, brethren, could not speak unto you as unto spiritual, but as unto carnal, even as unto babes in Christ. . . Ye were not able to bear it, neither yet now are ye able. For ye are yet carnal'. As a wise master-builder I have laid the foundation' and 'ye are the temple of God, and the Spirit of God dwelleth in you'. 'Let a man so account of us, as of the ministers of Christ, and stewards of the Mysteries of God'.

Can any one read this passage — and all that has been done in the summary is to bring out the salient points — without recognising the fact that the Apostle possessed a divine wisdom given in the Mysteries, that his Corinthian followers were not yet able to receive ? And note the recurring technical terms: the "wisdom", the "wisdom of God in a mystery", the "hidden wisdom", known only to the "spiritual" man; spoken of only among the "perfect", wisdom from which the non-"spiritual", the "babes in Christ", the "carnal", were excluded, known to the "wise master builder", the "steward of the Mysteries of God".

Again and again he refers to these Mysteries. Writing to the Ephesian Christians he says that "by revelation", by the unveiling, had been "made known unto me the Mystery", and hence his "knowledge in the Mystery of Christ"; all might know of the "fellowship of the Mystery". Of this Mystery, he repeated to the Colossians, he was "made a minister", "the Mystery which hath been hid from ages and from generations, but now is made manifest to His saints"; not to the world, nor even to Christians, but only to the Holy Ones. To them was unveiled " the glory of this Mystery"; and what was it ? "Christ in you" — a significant phrase, which we shall see, in a moment, belonged to the life of the Initiate; thus ultimately must every man learn the wisdom, and become "perfect in Christ Jesus". These Colossians he bids pray "that God would open to us a door of utterance, to speak the mystery of Christ", a passage to which S. Clement refers as one in which the apostle "clearly reveals that knowledge belongs not to all". So also he writes to his loved Timothy, bidding him select his deacons from those who hold "the Mystery of the faith in a pure conscience", that great "Mystery of Godliness", that he had learned, knowledge of which was necessary for the teachers of the Church.

Now S. Timothy holds an important position, as representing the next generation of Christian teachers. He was a pupil of S. Paul, and was appointed by him to guide and rule a portion of the Church. He had been, we learn, initiated into the Mysteries by S. Paul himself, and reference is made to this, the technical phrases once more serving as a clue. "This charge I commit unto thee, son Timothy, according to the prophecies which went before on thee", the solemn benediction of the Initiator, who admitted the candidate; but not alone was the Initiator present: "Neglect not the gift that is in thee, which was given thee by prophecy, by the laying on of the hands of the Presbytery", of the Elder Brothers. And he reminds him to lay hold of that "eternal life, whereunto thou art also called, and hast professed a good profession before many witnesses" — the vow of the new Initiate pledged in the presence of the Elder Brothers, and of the assembly of Initiates. The knowledge then given was the sacred charge of which S. Paul cries out so forcibly: "0 Timothy, keep that which is committed to thy trust" — not the knowledge commonly possessed by Christians, as to which no special obligation lay upon S. Timothy, but the sacred deposit committed to his trust as an Initiate, and essential to the welfare of the Church. S. Paul later recurs again to this, laying stress on the supreme importance of the matter in a way that would be exaggerated had the knowledge been the common property of Christian men: "Hold fast the form of sound words which thou hast heard of me .... That good thing which was committed unto thee, keep by the Holy Ghost which dwelleth in us" — as serious an adjuration as human lips could frame. Further, it was his duty to provide for the due transmission of this sacred deposit, that it might be handed on to the future, and the Church might never be left without teachers: "The things that thou hast heard of me among many witnesses" — the sacred oral teachings given in the assembly of Initiates, who bore witness to the accuracy of the transmission — " the same commit thou to faithful men, who shall be able to teach others also".

The knowledge — or, if the phrase be preferred, the supposition — that the Church possessed these hidden teachings throws a flood of light on the scattered remarks made by S. Paul about himself, and when they are gathered together, we have an outline of the evolution of the Initiate. S. Paul asserts that though he was already among the perfect, the Initiated — for he says: "Let us, therefore, as many as be perfect, be thus minded" — he had not yet "attained", was indeed not yet wholly "perfect", for he had not yet won Christ, he had not yet reached the "high calling of God in Christ", "the power of His resurrection, and the fellowship of His sufferings, being made conformable unto His death"; and he was striving, he says, "if by any means I might attain unto the resurrection of the dead". For this was the Initiation that liberated, that made the Initiate the Perfect Master, the Risen Christ, freeing Him finally from the "dead", from the humanity within the circle of generation, from the bonds that fettered the soul to gross matter. Here again we have a number of technical terms, and even the surface reader should realise that the "resurrection of the dead" here spoken of cannot be the ordinary resurrection of the modern Christian, supposed to be inevitable for all men, and therefore obviously not requiring any special struggle on the part of any one to attain to it. In fact the very word "attain" would be out of place in referring to a universal and inevitable human experience. S. Paul could not avoid that resurrection, according to the modern Christian view. What then was the resurrection to attain which he was making such strenuous efforts ? Once more the only answer comes from the Mysteries. In them the Initiate approaching the Initiation that liberated from the cycle of rebirth, the circle of generation, was called "the suffering Christ", he shared the sufferings of the Saviour of the world, was crucified mystically, "made conformable to His death," and then attained the resurrection, the fellowship of the glorified Christ, and, after, that death had over him no power. This was "the prize" towards which the great Apostle was pressing, and he urged "as many as be perfect", not the ordinary believer, thus also to strive. Let them not be content with what they had gained, but still press onwards.

This resemblance of the Initiate to the Christ is, indeed, the very groundwork of the Greater Mysteries, as we shall see more in detail when we study "The Mystical Christ". The Initiate was no longer to look on Christ as outside himself: "Though we have known Christ after the flesh, yet now henceforth know we Him no more".

The ordinary believer had "put on Christ", as many of you as have been baptised into Christ have put on Christ. Then they were the "babes in Christ" to whom reference has already been made, and Christ was the Saviour to whom they looked for help, knowing Him "after the flesh". But when they had conquered the lower nature and were no longer "carnal", then they were to enter on a higher path, and were themselves to become Christ. This which he himself had already reached, was the longing of the Apostle for his followers: "My little children, of whom I travail in birth again until Christ be formed in you." Already he was their spiritual father, having "begotten you through the gospel". But now "again" he was as a parent, as their mother to bring them to the second birth. Then the infant Christ, the Holy Child, was born in the soul, "the hidden man of the heart" the Initiate thus became that "Little Child"; henceforth he was to live out in his own person the life of the Christ, until he became the "perfect man", growing "unto the measure of the stature of the fullness of Christ". Then he, as S. Paul was doing, filled up the sufferings of Christ in his own flesh, and always bore "about in the body the dying of the Lord Jesus", so that he could truly say: "I am crucified with Christ: nevertheless I live; yet not I, but Christ liveth in me". Thus was the Apostle himself suffering; thus he describes himself. And when the struggle is over, how different is the calm tone of triumph from the strained effort of the earlier years: "I am now ready to be offered, and the time of my departure is at hand. I have fought a good fight, I have finished my course, I have kept the faith; henceforth there is laid up for me a crown of righteousness.' This was the crown given to "him that overcometh", of whom it is said by the ascended Christ: "I will make him a pillar in the temple of my God; and he shall go no more out". For after the "Resurrection" the Initiate has become the Perfect Man, the Master, and He goes out no more from the Temple, but from it serves and guides the worlds.

It may be well to point out, that S. Paul himself sanctions the use of the theoretical mystic teaching in explaining the historical events recorded in the Scriptures. The history therein written is not regarded by him as a mere record of facts, which occurred on the physical plane. A true mystic, he saw in the physical events the shadows of the universal truths ever unfolding in higher and inner worlds, and knew that the events selected for preservation in occult writings were such as were typical, the explanation of which would subserve human instruction. Thus he takes the story of Abraham, Sarai, Hagar, Ishmael, and Isaac, and saying, "which things are an allegory", he proceeds to give the mystical interpretation. Referring to the escape of the Israelites from Egypt, he speaks of the Red Sea as a baptism, of the manna and the water as spiritual meat and spiritual drink, of the rock from which the water flowed as Christ. He sees the great mystery of the union of Christ and His Church in the human relation of husband and wife, and speaks of Christians as the flesh and the bones of the body of Christ. The writer of the Epistle to the Hebrews allegorises the whole Jewish system of worship. In the Temple he sees a pattern of the heavenly

Temple, in the High Priest he sees Christ, in the sacrifices the offering of the spotless Son; the priests of the Temple are but "the example and shadow of heavenly things", of the heavenly priesthood serving in "the true tabernacle". A most elaborate allegory is thus worked out in chapters iii—x, and the writer alleges that the Holy Ghost thus signified the deeper meaning; all was "a figure for the time".

In this view of the sacred writings, it is not alleged that the events recorded did not take place, but only that their physical happening was a matter of minor importance. And such explanation is the unveiling of the Lesser Mysteries, the mystic teaching which is permitted to be given to the world. It is not, as many think, a mere play of the imagination, but is the outcome of a true intuition, seeing the patterns in the heavens, and not only the shadows cast by them on the screen of earthly time.

PART II

THE TESTIMONY OF THE CHURCH

While it may be that some would be willing to admit the possession by the Apostles and their immediate successors of a deeper knowledge of spiritual things than was current among the masses of the believers around them, few will probably be willing to take the next step, and, leaving that charmed circle, accept as the depository of their sacred learning the Mysteries of the Early Church. Yet we have S. Paul providing for the transmission of the unwritten teaching, himself initiating S. Timothy, and instructing S. Timothy to initiate others in his turn, who should again hand it on to yet others. We thus see the provision of four successive generations of teachers, spoken of in the Scriptures themselves, and these would far more than overlap the writers of the Early Church, who bear witness to the existence of the Mysteries. For among these are pupils of the Apostles themselves, though the most definite statements belong to those removed from the Apostles by one intermediate teacher. Now, as soon as we begin to study the writings of the Early Church, we are met by the facts that there are allusions which are only intelligible by the existence of the Mysteries, and then statements that the Mysteries are existing. This might, of course, have been expected, seeing the point at which the New Testament leaves the matter, but it is satisfactory to find the facts answer to the expectation.

The first witnesses are those called the Apostolic Fathers, the disciples of the Apostles; but very little of their writings, and that disputed, remains. Not being written controversially, the statements are not as categorical as those of the later writers. Their letters are for the encouragement of the believers. Polycarp, Bishop of Smyrna, and fellow-disciple with Ignatius of S. John, expresses a hope that his correspondents are " well versed in the sacred Scriptures and that nothing is hid from you; but to me this privilege is not yet granted" — writing, apparently, before reaching full Initiation. Barnabas speaks of communicating "some portion of what I have myself received", and after expounding the Law mystically, declares that "we then, rightly understanding His commandments, explain them as the Lord intended". Ignatius, Bishop of Antioch, a disciple of S. John, speaks of himself as "not yet perfect in Jesus Christ. For I now begin to be a disciple, and I speak to you as my fellow-disciples", and he speaks of them as "initiated into the mysteries of the Gospel with Paul, the holy, the martyred". Again he says: "Might I not write to you things more full of mystery ? But I fear to do so, lest I should inflict injury on you who are but babes. Pardon me in this respect, lest, as not being able to receive their weighty import, ye should be strangled by them. For even I, though I am bound [for Christ] and am able to understand heavenly things, the angelic orders, and the different sorts of angels and hosts, the distinction between powers and dominions, and the diversities between thrones and authorities, the mightiness of the eons, and the pre-eminence of the cherubim and seraphim, the sublimity of the Spirit, the kingdom of the Lord, and above all the incomparable majesty of Almighty God — though I am acquainted with these things, yet am I not therefore by any means perfect, nor am I such a disciple as Paul or Peter". This passage is interesting, as indicating that the organisation of the celestial hierarchies was one of the subjects in which instruction was given in the Mysteries. Again he speaks of the High Priest, the Hierophant, " to whom the holy of holies has been committed, and who alone has been entrusted with the secrets of God".

We come next to S. Clement of Alexandria and his pupil Origen, the two writers of the second and third centuries who tell us most about the Mysteries in the Early Church; though the general atmosphere is full of mystic allusions, these two are clear and categorical in their statements that the Mysteries were a recognised institution.

Now S. Clement was a disciple of Pantaenus, and he speaks of him and of two others, said to be probably Tatian and Theodotus, as "preserving the tradition of the blessed doctrine derived directly from the holy Apostles, Peter, James, John, and Paul', his link with the Apostles themselves consisting thus of only one intermediary. He was the head of the Catechetical School of Alexandria in A.D. 189, and died about A.D. 220. Origen, born about A.D. 185, was his pupil, and he is, perhaps, the most learned of the Fathers, and a man of the rarest moral beauty. These are the witnesses from whom we receive the most important testimony as to the existence of definite Mysteries in the Early Church.

The Stromata, or Miscellanies, of S. Clement are our source of information about the Mysteries in his time. He himself speaks of these writings as a "miscellany of Gnostic notes, according to the true philosophy", and also describes them as memoranda of the teachings he had himself received from Pantaenus. The passage is instructive: "The Lord . . . allowed us to communicate of those divine Mysteries, and of that holy light, to those who are able to receive them. He did not certainly disclose to the many what did not belong to the many; but to the few to whom He knew that they belonged, who were capable of receiving and being moulded according to them. But secret things are entrusted to speech, not to writing, as is the case with God. And if one say that it is written, ' There is nothing secret which shall not be revealed, nor hidden which shall not be disclosed,' let him also hear from us, that to him who hears secretly, even what is secret shall be manifested. This is what was predicted by this oracle. And to him who is able secretly to observe what is delivered to him, that which is veiled shall be disclosed as truth; and what is hidden to the many shall appear manifest to the few. . . . The Mysteries are delivered mystically, that what is spoken may be in the mouth of the speaker; rather not in his voice, but in his understanding . . . The writing of these memoranda of mine, I well know, is weak when compared with that spirit, full of grace, which I was privileged to hear. But it will be an image to recall the archetype to him who was struck with the Thyrsus." The Thyrsus, we may here interject, was the wand borne by Initiates, and candidates were touched with it during the ceremony of Initiation. It had a mystic significance, symbolising the spinal cord and the pineal gland in the Lesser Mysteries, and a Rod, known to Occultists, in the Greater. To say, therefore, "to him who was struck with the Thyrsus" was exactly the same as to say, "to him who was initiated in the Mysteries". Clement proceeds: "We profess not to explain secret things sufficiently — far from it — but only to recall them to memory, whether we have forgot aught, or whether for the purpose of not forgetting. Many things, I well know, have escaped us, through length of time, that have dropped away unwritten. . . . There are then some things of which we have no recollection; for the power that was in the blessed men was great". A frequent experience of those taught by the Great Ones, for Their presence stimulates and renders active powers which are normally latent, and which the pupil, unassisted, cannot evoke. "There are also some things which remained unnoted long, which have now escaped; and others which are effaced, having faded away in the mind itself, since such a task is not easy to those not experienced; these I revive in my commentaries. Some things I purposely omit, in the exercise of a wise selection, afraid to write what I guarded against speaking; not grudging — for that were wrong — but fearing for my readers, lest they should stumble by taking them in a wrong sense; and, as the proverb says, we should be found "reaching a sword to a child". For it is impossible that what has been written should not escape [become known], although remaining unpublished by me. But being always revolved, using the one only voice, that of writing, they answer nothing to him that makes enquiries beyond what is written; for they require of necessity the aid of some one, either of him who wrote, or of some one else who has walked in his footsteps. Some things my treatise will hint; on some it will linger; some it will merely mention. It will try to speak imperceptibly, to exhibit secretly, and to demonstrate silently".

This passage, if it stood alone, would suffice to establish the existence of a secret teaching in the Early Church. But it stands by no means alone. In Chapter xii of this same Book I, headed, "The Mysteries of the Faith not to be divulged to all" Clement declares that, since others than the wise may see his work, "it is requisite, therefore to hide in a Mystery the wisdom spoken, which the Son of God taught". Purified tongue of the speaker, purified ears of the hearer, these were necessary. "Such were the impediments in the way of my writing. And even now I fear, as it is said to cast the pearls before swine, lest they tread them under foot and turn and rend us ' For it is difficult to exhibit the really pure and transparent words respecting the true light, to swinish and untrained hearers. For scarcely could anything which they could hear be more ludicrous than these to the multitude; nor any subjects on the other hand more admirable or more inspiring to those of noble nature. But the wise do not utter with their mouth what they reason in council. But what ye hear in the ear said the Lord, 'proclaim upon the houses' bidding them receive the secret traditions of the true knowledge, and expound them aloft and conspicuously; and as we have heard in the

31

ear" so to deliver them to whom it is requisite; but not enjoining us to communicate to all without distinction, what is said to them in parables. But there is only a delineation in the memoranda, which have the truth sown sparse and broadcast, that it may escape the notice of those who pick up seeds like jackdaws; but when they find a good husbandman, each one of them will germinate and will produce corn".

Clement might have added that to "proclaim upon the houses" was to proclaim or expound in the assembly of the Perfect, the Initiated, and by no means to shout aloud to the man in the street.

Again he says that those who are "still blind and dumb, not having understanding, or the un-dazzled and keen vision of the contemplative soul . . . must stand outside of the divine choir. . . . Wherefore, in accordance with the method of concealment, the truly sacred Word, truly divine and most necessary for us, deposited in the shrine of truth, was by the Egyptians indicated by what were called among them adyta, and by the Hebrews by the veil. Only the consecrated . . . were allowed access to them. For Plato also thought it not lawful for ' the impure to touch the pure. Thence the prophecies and oracles are spoken in enigmas, and the Mysteries are not exhibited incontinently to all and sundry, but only after certain purifications and previous instructions". He then descants at great length on Symbols, expounding Pythagorean, Hebrew, Egyptian, and then remarks that the ignorant and unlearned man fails in understanding them. "But the Gnostic apprehends. Now then it is not wished that all things should be exposed indiscriminately to all and sundry, or the benefits of wisdom communicated to those who have not even in a dream been purified in soul (for it is not allowed to hand to every chance comer what has been procured with such laborious efforts); nor are the Mysteries of the Word to be expounded to the profane". The Pythagoreans and Plato, Zeno, and Aristotle had exoteric and esoteric teachings. The philosophers established the Mysteries, for "was it not more beneficial for the holy and blessed contemplation of realities to be concealed?" The Apostles also approved of "veiling the Mysteries of the Faith", "for there is an instruction to the perfect", alluded to in Colossians i, 9-11 and 25-27. "So that, on the one hand, then, there are the Mysteries which were hid till the time of the Apostles, and were delivered by them as they were received from the Lord, and, concealed in the Old Testament, were manifested to the saints. And, on the other hand, there is ' the riches of the glory of the mystery in the Gentiles,' which is faith and hope in Christ; which in another place he has called the ' foundation'". He quotes S. Paul to show that this "knowledge belongs not to all", and says, referring to Heb. v. and vi., that "there were certainly among the Hebrews, some things delivered unwritten"; and then refers to S. Barnabas, who speaks of God, "who has put into our hearts wisdom and the understanding of His secrets", and says that "it is but for few to comprehend these things", as showing a "trace of Gnostic tradition". "Wherefore instruction, which reveals hidden things, is called illumination, as it is the teacher only who uncovers the lid of the ark". Further referring to S. Paul, he comments on his remark to the Romans that he will "come in the fullness of the blessing of Christ," and says that he thus designates "the spiritual gift and the Gnostic interpretation, which being present he desires to impart to them present as ' the fullness of Christ, according to the revelation of the Mystery sealed in the ages of eternity, but now manifested by the prophetic Scriptures' .....But only to a few of them is shown what those things are which are contained in the Mystery. Rightly, then, Plato, in the epistles, treating of God, says: ' We must speak in enigmas; that should the tablet come by any mischance on its leaves either by sea or land, he who reads may remain ignorant'."

After much examination of Greek writers, and an investigation into philosophy, S. Clement declares that the Gnosis "imparted and revealed by the Son of God, is wisdom. . . . And the Gnosis itself is that which has descended by transmission to a few, having been imparted unwritten by the Apostles". A very long exposition of the life of the Gnostic, the Initiate, is given, and S. Clement concludes it by saying: "Let the specimen suffice to those who have ears. For it is not required to unfold the mystery, but only to indicate what is sufficient for those who are partakers in knowledge to bring it to mind".

Regarding Scripture as consisting of allegories and symbols, and as hiding the sense in order to stimulate enquiry and to preserve the ignorant from danger. S. Clement naturally confined the higher instruction to the learned. "Our Gnostic will be deeply learned", he says. "Now the Gnostic must be erudite". Those who had acquired readiness by previous training could master the deeper knowledge, for though "a man can be a believer without learning, so also we assert that it is impossible for a man without learning to comprehend the things which are declared in the faith". "Some who think themselves naturally gifted, do not wish to touch either philosophy or logic; nay more, they do not wish to learn natural science. They demand bare faith alone. . . So also I call him truly learned who brings everything to bear on the truth — so that, from geometry, and music, and grammar, and philosophy itself, culling what is useful, he guards the faith against assault. How necessary is it for him who desires to be partaker of the power of God, to treat of intellectual subjects by philosophising". "The Gnostic avails himself of branches of learning as auxiliary preparatory exercise." So far was S. Clement from thinking that the teaching of Christianity should be measured by the ignorance of the unlearned. "He who is conversant with all kinds of wisdom will be pre-eminently a Gnostic". Thus while he welcomed the ignorant and the sinner, and found in the Gospel what was suited to their needs, he considered that only the learned and the pure were fit candidates for the Mysteries. "The Apostle, in contradistinction to Gnostic perfection, calls the common faith the foundation, and sometimes milk", but on that foundation the edifice of the Gnosis was to be raised, and the food of men was to succeed that of babes. There is nothing of harshness nor of contempt in the distinction he draws, but only a calm and wise recognition of the facts.

Even the well-prepared candidate, the learned and trained pupil, could only hope to advance step by step in the profound truths unveiled in the Mysteries. This appears clearly in his comments on the vision of Hennas, in which he also throws out some hints on methods of reading occult works. "Did not the Power also, that appeared to Hermas in the Vision, in the form of the Church, give for transcription the book which she wished to be made known to the elect ? And this, he says, he transcribed to the letter, without finding how to complete the syllables. And this signified that the Scripture is clear to all, when taken according to base reading; and that this is the faith which occupies the place of the rudiments. Wherefore also the figurative expression is employed, 'reading according to the letter', while we understand that the gnostic unfolding of Scriptures, when faith has already reached an advanced state, is likened to reading according to the syllables . . . Now that the Saviour has taught the Apostles, the unwritten rendering of the written (scriptures) has been handed down also to us, inscribed by the power of God on hearts new, according to the renovation of the book. Thus those of highest repute among the Greeks dedicate the fruit of the pomegranate to Hermes, who they say is speech, on account of its interpretation. For speech conceals much. . . . That it is therefore not only to those who read simply that the acquisition of the truth is so difficult, but that not even to those whose prerogative the knowledge of the truth is, is the contemplation of it vouchsafed all at once, the history of Moses teaches; until accustomed to gaze, as the Hebrews on the glory of Moses, and the prophets of Israel on the visions of angels, so we also become able to look the splendours of truth in the face.'

Yet more references might be given, but these should suffice to establish the fact that S. Clement knew of, had been initiated into, and wrote for the benefit of those who had also been initiated into, the Mysteries in the Church.

The next witness is his pupil Origen, that most shining light of learning, courage, sanctity, devotion, meekness, and zeal, whose works remain as mines of gold wherein the student may dig for the treasures of wisdom.

In his famous controversy with Celsus attacks were made on Christianity which drew out a defence of the Christian position in which frequent references were made to the secret teachings.

Celsus had alleged, as a matter of attack, that Christianity was a secret system, and Origen traverses this by saying that while certain doctrines were secret, many others were public, and that this system of exoteric and esoteric teachings, adopted in Christianity, was also in general use among philosophers. The reader should note, in the following passage, the distinction drawn between the resurrection of Jesus, regarded in a historical light, and the "mystery of the resurrection".

"Moreover, since he [Celsus] frequently calls the Christian doctrine a secret system [of belief], we must confute him on this point also, since almost the entire world is better acquainted with what Christians preach than with the favourite opinions of philosophers. For who is ignorant of the statement that Jesus was born of a virgin, and that He was crucified, and that His resurrection is an article of faith among many, and that a general judgment is announced to come, in which the wicked are to be punished according to their deserts, and the righteous to be duly rewarded? And yet the Mystery of the resurrection, not being understood, is made a subject of ridicule among unbelievers. In these circumstances, to speak of the Christian doctrine as a secret system, is altogether absurd. But that there should be certain doctrines, not made known to the multitude, which are [revealed] after the exoteric ones have been taught, is not a peculiarity of Christianity alone, but also of philosophic systems, in which certain truths are exoteric and others esoteric. Some of the hearers of Pythagoras were content with his ipse dixit; while others were taught in secret those doctrines which were not deemed fit to be communicated to profane and insufficiently prepared ears. Moreover, all the Mysteries that are celebrated everywhere throughout Greece and barbarous countries, although held in secret, have no discredit thrown upon them, so that it is in vain he endeavours to calumniate the secret doctrines of Christianity, seeing that he does not correctly understand its nature".

It is impossible to deny that, in this important passage, Origen distinctly places the Christian Mysteries in the same category as those of the Pagan world, and claims that what is not regarded as a discredit to other religions should not form a subject of attack when found in Christianity.

Still writing against Celsus, he declares that the secret teachings of Jesus were preserved in the Church, and refers specifically to the explanations that He gave to His disciples of His parables, in answering Celsus' comparison of "the inner Mysteries of the Church of God" with the Egyptian worship of Animals. " I have not yet spoken of the observance of all that is written in the Gospels, each one of which contains much doctrine difficult to be understood, not merely by the multitude, but even by certain of the more intelligent, including a very profound explanation of the parables which Jesus delivered to ' those without,' while reserving the exhibition of their full meaning for those who had passed beyond the stage of exoteric teaching, and who came to Him privately in the house. And when he comes to understand it, he will admire the reason why some are said to be' without,' and others ' in the house.'

And he refers guardedly to the "mountain" which Jesus ascended, from which he came down again to help "those who were unable to follow Him whither His disciples went". The allusion is to "the Mountain of Initiation", a well-known mystical phrase, as Moses also made the Tabernacle after the pattern "showed thee in the mount". Origen refers to it again later, saying that Jesus showed himself to be very different in his real appearance when on the "Mountain", from what those saw who could not " follow Him so high."

So also, in his commentary on the Gospel of Matthew, Chap, xv, dealing with the episode of the Syro-Phoenician woman, Origen remarks: "And perhaps, also, of the words of Jesus there are some loaves which it is possible to give to the more rational, as to children, only; and others as it were crumbs from the great house and table of the well-born, which may be used by some souls like dogs".

Celsus complaining that sinners were brought into the Church, Origen answers that the Church had medicine for those that were sick, but also the study and the knowledge of divine things for those who were in health. Sinners were taught not to sin, and only when it was seen that progress had been made, and men were "purified by the Word", "then, and not before, do we invite them to participation in our Mysteries. For we speak wisdom among them that are perfect". Sinners came to be healed: "For there are in the divinity of the Word some helps towards the cure of those who are sick. . . . Others, again, which to the pure in soul and body exhibit the ' revelation of the Mystery, which was kept secret since the world began, but now is made manifest by the Scriptures of the prophets,' and ' by the appearing of our Lord Jesus Christ,' which 'appearing' is manifested to each one of those who are perfect, and which enlightens the reason in the true knowledge of things". Such appearances of divine Beings took place, we have seen, in the Pagan Mysteries, and those of the Church had equally glorious visitants. "God the Word", he says, "was sent as a physician to sinners, but as a Teacher of Divine Mysteries to those who are already pure, and who sin no more". "Wisdom will not enter into the soul of a base man, nor dwell in a body that is involved in sin;" hence these higher teachings are given only to those who are "athletes in piety and in every virtue".

Christians did not admit the impure to this knowledge, but said: "Whoever has clean hands, and, therefore, lifts up holy hands to God .. . let him come to us .... whoever is pure not only from all defilement, but from what are regarded as lesser transgressions, let him be boldly initiated in the Mysteries of Jesus, which properly are made known only to the holy and the pure". Hence also, ere the ceremony of Initiation began, he who acts as Initiator, according to the precepts of Jesus, the Hierophant, made the significant proclamation "to those who have been purified in heart: He, whose soul has, for a long time, been conscious of no evil, especially since he yielded himself to the healing of the Word, let such a one hear the doctrines which were spoken in private by Jesus to His genuine disciples". This was the opening of the "initiating those who were already purified into the sacred Mysteries". Such only might learn the realities of the unseen worlds, and might enter into the sacred precincts where, as of old, angels were the teachers, and where knowledge was given by sight and not only by words. It is impossible not to be struck with the different tone of these Christians from that of their modern successors. With them perfect purity of life, the practice of virtue, the fulfilling of the divine Law in every detail of outer conduct, the perfection of righteousness, were — as with the Pagans — only the beginning of the way instead of the end. Nowadays religion is considered to have gloriously accomplished its object when it has made the Saint; then, it was to the Saints that it devoted its highest energies, and, taking the pure in heart, it led them to the Beatific Vision.

The same fact of secret teaching comes out again, when Origen is discussing the arguments of Celsus as to the wisdom of retaining ancestral customs, based on the belief that "the various quarters of the earth were from the beginning allotted to different superintending Spirits, and were thus distributed among certain governing Powers, and in this way the administration of the world is carried on".

Origen having animadverted on the deductions of Celsus, proceeds: "But as we think it likely that some of those who are accustomed to deeper investigation will fall in with this treatise, let us venture to lay down some considerations of a profounder kind, conveying a mystical and secret view respecting the original distribution of the various quarters of the earth among different superintending Spirits". He says that Celsus has misunderstood the deeper reasons relating to the arrangement of terrestrial affairs, some of which are even touched upon in Grecian history. Then he quotes Deut., xxxii, 8-9: "When the Most High divided the nations, when he dispersed the sons of Adam, He set the bounds of the people according to the number of the Angels of God; and the Lord's portion was his people Jacob, and Israel the cord of his inheritance". This is the wording of the Septuagint, not that of the English authorised version, but it is very suggestive of the title, the "Lord", being regarded as that of the Ruling Angel of the Jews only, and not of the "Most High", i.e., God. This view has disappeared, from ignorance, and hence the impropriety of many of the statements referring to the "Lord", when they are transferred to the "Most High", e.g., Judges, i,19.

Origen then relates the history of the Tower of Babel, and continues: "But on these subjects much, and that of a mystical kind, might be said; in keeping with which is the following:' It is good to keep close the secret of a king,' Tobit, xii, 7, in order that the doctrine of the entrance of souls into bodies (not, however, that of the transmigration from one body into another) may not be thrown before the common understanding, nor what is holy given to the dogs, nor pearls be cast before swine. For such a procedure would be impious, being equivalent to a betrayal of the mysterious declarations of God's wisdom ... It is sufficient, however, to represent in the style of a historic narrative what is intended to convey a secret meaning in the garb of history, that those who have the capacity may work out for themselves all that relates to the subject". He then expounds more fully the Tower of Babel story, and writes: "Now, in the next place, if any one has the capacity let him understand that in what assumes the form of history, and which contains some things that are literally true, while yet it conveys a deeper meaning. . . ."

After endeavouring to show that the "Lord" was more powerful than the other superintending Spirits of the different quarters of the earth, and that he sent his people forth to be punished by living under the dominion of the other powers, and afterwards reclaimed them with all of the less favoured nations who could be drawn in, Origen concludes by saying: "As we have previously observed, these remarks are to be understood as being made by us with a concealed meaning, by way of pointing out the mistakes of those who assert. . . ." as did Celsus.

After remarking that " the object of Christianity is that we should become wise", Origen proceeds: "If you come to the books written after the time of Jesus, you will find that those multitudes of believers who hear the parables are, as it were, ' without,' and worthy only of exoteric doctrines, while the disciples learn in private the explanation of the parables. For, privately, to His own disciples did Jesus open up all things, esteeming above the multitudes those who desired to know His wisdom. And He promises to those who believe on Him to send them wise men and scribes. . . . And Paul also in the catalogue of 'Charismata' bestowed by God, placed first 'the Word of wisdom', and second, as being inferior to it,' the word of knowledge,' but third, and lower down, 'faith'. And because he regarded 'the Word' as higher than miraculous powers, he for that reason places 'workings of miracles' and 'gifts of healings' in a lower place than gifts of the Word".

The Gospel truly helped the ignorant, "but it is no hindrance to the knowledge of God, but an assistance, to have been educated, and to have studied the best opinions, and to be wise". As for the unintelligent, "I endeavour to improve such also to the best of my ability, although I would not desire to build up the Christian community out of such materials. For I seek in preference those who are more clever and acute, because they are able to comprehend the meaning of the hard sayings". Here we have plainly stated the ancient Christian idea, entirely at one with the considerations submitted. There is room for the ignorant in Christianity, but it is not intended only for them, and has deep teachings for the "clever and acute".

It is for these that he takes much pains to show that the Jewish and Christian Scriptures have hidden meanings, veiled under stories the outer meaning of which repels them as absurd, alluding to the serpent and the tree of life, and "the other statements which follow, which might of themselves lead a candid reader to see that all these things had, not inappropriately, an allegorical meaning". Many chapters are devoted to these allegorical and mystical meanings, hidden beneath the words of the Old and New Testaments, and he alleges that Moses, like the Egyptians, gave histories with concealed meanings". "He who deals candidly with histories" — this is Origen's general canon of interpretation — "and would wish to keep himself also from being imposed on by them, will exercise his judgment as to what statements he will give his assent to, and what he will accept figuratively, seeking to discover the meaning of the authors of such inventions, and from what statements he will withhold his beliefs, as having been written for the gratification of certain individuals. And we have said this by way of anticipation respecting the whole history related in the Gospels concerning Jesus". A great part of his Fourth Book is taken up with illustrations of the mystical explanations of the Scripture stories, and anyone who wishes to pursue the subject can read through it.

In the De Principiis, Origen gives it as the received teaching of the Church " that the Scriptures were written by the Spirit of God, and have a meaning, not only such as is apparent at first sight, but also another, which escapes the notice of most. For those [words] which are written are the forms of certain Mysteries, and the images of divine things. Respecting which there is one opinion throughout the whole Church, that the whole law is indeed spiritual; but that the spiritual meaning which the law conveys is not known to all, but to those only on whom the grace of the Holy Spirit is bestowed in the word of wisdom and knowledge". Those who remember what has already been quoted will see in the "Word of wisdom" and "the word of knowledge" the two typical mystical instructions, the spiritual and the intellectual.

In the Fourth Book of De Principiis, Origen explains at length his views on the interpretation of Scripture. It has a "body", which is the "common and historical sense"; a "soul", a figurative meaning to be discovered by the exercise of the intellect; and a " spirit," an inner and divine sense, to be known only by those who have "the mind of Christ". He considers that incongruous and impossible things are introduced into the history to arouse an intelligent reader, and compel him to search for a deeper explanation, while simple people would read on without appreciating the difficulties.

Cardinal Newman, in his Arians of the Fourth Century, has some interesting remarks on the Disciplina Arcani, but, with the deeply-rooted ingrained scepticism of the nineteenth century, he cannot believe to the full in the "riches of the glory of the Mystery", or probably never for a moment conceived the possibility of the existence of such splendid realities. Yet he was a believer in Jesus, and the words of the promise of Jesus were clear and definite: "I will not leave you comfortless; I will come to you. Yet a little while, and the world seeth me no more; but ye see me: because I live, ye shall live also. At that day ye shall know that I am in my Father, and ye in me, and I in you". The promise was amply redeemed, for He came to them and taught them in His Mysteries; therein they saw Him, though the world saw Him no more, and they knew the Christ as in them, and their life as Christ's.

Cardinal Newman recognises a secret tradition, handed down from the Apostles, but he considers that it consisted of Christian doctrines, later divulged, forgetting that those who were told that they were not yet fit to receive it were not heathen, nor even catechumens under instruction, but full communicating members of the Christian Church. Thus he states that this secret tradition was later "authoritatively divulged and perpetuated in the form of symbols", and was embodied "in the creeds of the early Councils". But as the doctrines in the creeds are to be found clearly stated in the Gospels and Epistles, this position is wholly untenable, all these having been already divulged to the world at large; and in all of them the members of the Church were certainly thoroughly instructed. The repeated statements as to secrecy become meaningless if thus explained. The Cardinal, however, says that whatever "has not been thus authenticated, whether it was prophetical information or comment on the past dispensations, is, from the circumstances of the case, lost to the Church". That is very probably, in fact, certainly, true, so far as the Church is concerned, but it is none the less recoverable.

Commenting on Ireneeus, who in his work Against Heresies lays much stress on the existence of an Apostolic Tradition in the Church, the Cardinal writes: "He then proceeds to speak of the clearness and cogency of the traditions preserved in the Church, as containing that true wisdom of the perfect, of which S. Paul speaks, and to which the Gnostics pretended. And, indeed, without formal proofs of the existence and the authority in primitive times of an Apostolic Tradition, it is plain that there must have been such a tradition, granting that the Apostles conversed, and their friends had memories, like other men. It is quite inconceivable that they should not have been led to arrange the series of revealed doctrines more systematically than they record them in Scripture, as soon as their converts became exposed to the attacks and misrepresentations of heretics; unless they were forbidden to do so, a supposition which cannot be maintained. Their statements thus occasioned would be preserved as a matter of course; together with those other secret but less important truths, to which S. Paul seems to allude, and which the early writers more or less acknowledge, whether concerning the types of the Jewish Church, or the prospective fortunes of the Christian. And such recollections of apostolical teaching would evidently be binding on the faith of those who were instructed in them; unless it can be supposed that, though coming from inspired teachers, they were not of divine origin". In a part of the section dealing with the allegorising method, he writes in reference to the sacrifice of Isaac, etc., as "typical of the New Testament revelation": "In corroboration of this remark, let it be observed, that there seems to have been in the Church a traditionary explanation of these historical types, derived from the Apostles, but kept among the secret doctrines, as being dangerous to the majority of hearers; and certainly S. Paul, in the Epistle to the Hebrews, affords us an instance of such a tradition, both as existing and as secret (even though it be shown to be of Jewish origin), when, first checking himself and questioning his brethren's faith, he communicates, not without hesitation, the evangelical scope of the account of Melchisedec, as introduced into the book of Genesis".

The social and political convulsions that accompanied its dying now began to torture the vast frame of the Roman Empire, and even the Christians were caught up in the whirlpool of selfish warring interests. We still find scattered references to special knowledge imparted to the leaders and teachers of the Church, knowledge of the heavenly hierarchies, instructions given by angels, and so on. But the lack of suitable pupils caused the Mysteries to be withdrawn as an institution publicly known to exist, and teaching was given more and more secretly to those rarer and rarer souls, who by learning, purity, and devotion showed themselves capable of receiving it. No longer were schools to be found wherein the preliminary teachings were given, and with the disappearance of these the "door was shut".

Two streams may nevertheless be tracked through Christendom, streams which had as their source the vanished Mysteries. One was the stream of mystic learning, flowing from the Wisdom, the Gnosis, imparted in the Mysteries; the other was the stream of mystic contemplation, equally part of the Gnosis, leading to the ecstasy, to spiritual vision. This latter, however, divorced from knowledge, rarely attained the true ecstasies, and tended either to run riot in the lower regions of the invisible worlds, or to lose itself amid a variegated crowd of subtle superphysical forms, visible as objective appearances to the inner vision — prematurely forced by fastings, vigils, and strained attention — but mostly born of the thoughts and emotions of the seer. Even when the forms observed were not externalised thoughts, they were seen through a distorting atmosphere of preconceived ideas and beliefs, and were thus rendered largely unreliable. None the less, some of the visions were verily of heavenly things, and Jesus truly appeared from time to time to His devoted lovers, and angels would sometimes brighten with their presence the cell of monk and nun, the solitude of rapt devotee and patient seeker after God. To deny the possibility of such experiences would be to strike at the very root of that "which has been most surely believed" in all religions, and is known to all Occultists — the intercommunication between Spirits veiled in flesh and those clad in subtler vestures, the touching of mind with mind across the barriers of matter, the unfolding of the Divinity in man, the sure knowledge of a life beyond the gates of death.

Glancing down the centuries we find no time in which Christendom was left wholly devoid of mysteries. "It was probably about the end of the 5th century, just as ancient philosophy was dying out in the Schools of Athens, that the speculative philosophy of neo-Platonism made a definite lodgment in Christian thought through the literary forgeries of the Pseudo-Dionysius. The doctrines of Christianity were by that time so firmly established that the Church could look upon a symbolical or mystical interpretation of them without anxiety. The author of the Theologica Mystica and the other works ascribed to the Areopagite proceeds, therefore, to develop the doctrines of Proclus with very little modification into a system of esoteric Christianity. God is the nameless and supra-essential One, elevated above goodness itself. Hence 'negative theology', which ascends from the creature to God by dropping one after another every determinate predicate, leads us nearest to the truth. The return to God is the consummation of all things and the goal indicated by Christian teaching. The same doctrines were preached with more of churchly fervour by Maximus, the Confessor, (580-622). Maximus represents almost the last speculative activity of the Greek Church, but the influence of the Pseudo-Dionysian writing was transmitted to the West in the ninth century by Erigena, in whose speculative spirit both the scholasticism and the mysticism of the Middle Ages have their rise. Erigena translated Dionysius into Latin along with the commentaries of Maximus, and his system is essentially based upon theirs. The negative theology is adopted, and God is stated to be predicateless Being, above all categories, and therefore not improperly called Nothing [query, No-Thing]. Out of this Nothing or incomprehensible essence the world of ideas or primordial causes is eternally created. This is the Word or Son of God, in whom all things exist, so far as they have substantial existence. All existence is a theophany, and as God is the beginning of all things, so also is He the end. Erigena teaches the restitution of all things under the form of the Dionysian adunatio or deificatio. These are the permanent outlines of what may be called the philosophy of mysticism in Christian times, and it is remarkable with how little variation they are repeated from age to age".

In the eleventh century Bernard of Clairvaux (A.D. 1091-1153) and Hugo of S. Victor carry on the mystic tradition, with Richard of S. Victor in the following century, and S. Bonaventura the Seraphic Doctor, and the great S. Thomas Aquinas (A.D. 1227-1274) in the thirteenth. Thomas Aquinas dominates the Europe of the Middle Ages, by his force of character no less than by his learning and piety. He asserts "Revelation" as one source of knowledge, Scripture and tradition being the two channels in which it runs, and the influence, seen in his writings, of the Pseudo-Dionysius links him to the Neo-Platonists. The second source is Reason, and here the channels are the Platonic philosophy and the methods of Aristotle — the latter an alliance that did Christianity no good, for Aristotle became an obstacle to the advance of the higher thought, as was made manifest in the struggles of Giordano Bruno, the Pythagorean. Thomas Aquinas was canonised in A.D. 1323, and the great Dominican remains as a type of the union of theology and philosophy — the aim of his life. These belong to the great Church of western Europe, vindicating her claim to be regarded as the transmitter of the holy torch of mystic learning. Around her there also sprang up many sects, deemed heretical, yet containing true traditions of the sacred secret learning, the Cathari and many others, persecuted by a Church jealous of her authority, and fearing lest the holy pearls should pass into profane custody. In this century also S. Elizabeth of Hungary shines out with sweetness and purity, while Eckhart (A.D. 1260-1329) proves himself a worthy inheritor of the Alexandrian Schools. Eckhart taught that "the Godhead is the absolute Essence (Wesen), unknowable not only by man but also by Itself; It is darkness and absolute indeterminateness, Nicht in contrast to Icht, or definite and knowable existence. Yet It is the potentiality of all things, and Its nature is, in a triadic process, to come to consciousness of Itself as the triune God. Creation is not a temporal act, but an eternal necessity, of the divine nature. I am as necessary to God, Eckhart is fond of saying, as God is necessary tome. In my knowledge and love God knows and loves Himself".

Eckhart is followed, in the fourteenth century, by John Tauler, and Nicolas of Basel, "the Friend of God in the Oberland". From these sprang up the Society of the Friends of God, true mystics and followers of the old tradition. Mead remarks that Thomas Aquinas, Tauler, and Eckhart followed the Pseudo-Dionysius, who followed Plotinus, Iamblichus, and Proclus, who in turn followed Plato and Pythagoras. So linked together are the followers of the Wisdom in all ages. It was probably a "Friend" who was the author of Die Deutsche Theologie, a book of mystical devotion, which had the curious fortune of being approved by Staupitz, the Vicar-General of the Augustiman Order, who recommended it to Luther and by Luther himself, who published it A.D. 1516, as a book which should rank immediately after the Bible and the writings of S. Augustine of Hippo. Another "Friend" was Ruysbroeck, to whose influence with Groot was due the founding of the Brethren of the Common Lot or Common Life —a Society that must remain ever memorable, as it numbered among its members that prince of mystics, Thomas a Kempis (A. D. 1380-1471), the author of the immortal Imitation of Christ.

In the fifteenth century the more purely intellectual side of mysticism comes out more strongly than the ecstatic — so dominant in these societies of the fourteenth — and we have Cardinal Nicolas of Cusa, with Giordano Bruno, the martyred knight-errant of philosophy, and Paracelsus, the much slandered scientist, who drew his knowledge directly from the original eastern fountain, instead of through Greek channels.

The sixteenth century saw the birth of Jacob Bohme (A.D. 1575-1624), the "inspired cobbler", an Initiate in obscuration truly, sorely persecuted by unenlightened men; and then too came S. Teresa, the much-oppressed and suffering Spanish mystic; and S. John of the Cross, a burning flame of intense devotion; and S. Francois de Sales. Wise was Rome in canonising these, wiser than the Reformation that persecuted Böhme, but the spirit of the Reformation was ever intensely anti-mystical, and wherever its breath hath passed the fair flowers of mysticism have withered as under the sirocco.

Borne, however, who, though she canonised Teresa dead, had sorely harried her while living — did ill with Mme. de Guyon (A. D. 1648-1717), a true mystic, and with Miguel de Molinos (1627-1696), worthy to sit near S. John of the Cross, who carried on in the seventeenth century the high devotion of the mystic, turned into a peculiarly passive form — the Quietist.

In this same century arose the school of Platonists in Cambridge, of whom Henry More (A. D. 1614-1687) may serve as salient example; also Thomas Vaughan, and Robert Fludd the Rosicrucian; and there is formed also the Philadelphian Society, and we see William Law (A.D. 1686-1761) active in the eighteenth century, and overlapping S. Martin (A. D. 1743-1803), whose writings have fascinated so many nineteenth century students.

Nor should we omit Christian Rosenkreutz (d. A.D. 1484), whose mystic Society of the Rosy Cross, appearing in 1614, held true knowledge, and whose spirit was reborn in the "Comte de S. Germain", the mysterious figure that appears and disappears through the gloom, lit by lurid flashes, of the closing eighteenth century. Mystics too were some of the Quakers, the much-persecuted sect of Friends, seeking the illumination of the Inner Light, and listening ever for the Inner Voice. And many another mystic was there, "of whom the world was not worthy", like the wholly delightful and wise Mother Juliana of Norwich, of the fourteenth century, jewels of Christendom, too little known, but justifying Christianity to the world.

Yet, as we salute reverently these Children of the Light, scattered over the centuries, we are forced to recognise in them the absence of that union of acute intellect and high devotion which were welded together by the training of the Mysteries, and while we marvel that they soared so high, we cannot but wish that their rare gifts had been developed under that magnificent disciplina arcani.

Alphonse Louis Constant, better known under his pseudonym, Eliphas Levi, has put rather well the loss of the Mysteries, and the need for their re-institution. "A great misfortune befell Christianity. The betrayal of the Mysteries by the false

Gnostics — for the Gnostics, that is, those who know, were the Initiates of primitive Christianity — caused the Gnosis to be rejected, and alienated the Church from the supreme truths of the Kabbala, which contain all the secrets of transcendental theology .... Let the most absolute science, let the highest reason, become once more the patrimony of the leaders of the people; let the sacerdotal art and the royal art take the double sceptre of antique initiations, and the social world will once more issue from its chaos. Burn the holy images no longer; demolish the temples no more; temples and images are necessary for men; but drive the hirelings from the house of prayer; let the blind be no longer leaders of the blind, reconstruct the hierarchy of intelligence and holiness, and recognise only those who know as the teachers of those who believe".

Will the Churches of today again take up the mystic teaching, the Lesser Mysteries, and so prepare their children for the re-establishment of the Greater Mysteries, again drawing down the Angels as Teachers, and having as Hierophant the Divine Master, Jesus? On the answer to that question depends the future of Christianity.

www.ingramcontent.com/pod-product-compliance
Lightning Source LLC
LaVergne TN
LVHW041500070426
835507LV00009B/722